HEAVY METAL FUN TIME ACTIVITY BOX

ECW Press

Published by ECW PRESS
2120 Queen Street East, Suite 200, Toronto, Ontario, Canada M4E 1E2

LIBRARY AND ARCHIVES CANADA CATALOGUING IN PUBLICATION

Morano, Aye Jay
Heavy metal fun time activity book / Aye Jay Morano

ISBN: 978-1-55022-798-7

1. Heavy metal (Music) — Humor. I. Title

ML3534.M829 2007   782.421660207   C2007-902589-7

Developing editor: Jennifer Hale
Cover and text design: Aye Jay
Typesetting: Rachel Ironstone
Printing: Webcom   4 5

MIX
Paper from
responsible sources
FSC® C004071

PRINTED AND BOUND IN CANADA

ECW PRESS
ecwpress.com

Joy and Celebration: A Foreword

By Andrew W.K.

For those already familiar with me, "Hello." For those unfamiliar with me, "You're now already more familiar with me than you had been prior to picking up this book and beginning to read this introduction." I've recorded several songs you may have heard, including, "Party Hard," "We Want Fun," and "It's Time To Party." I now want to ask you, "What does the word 'party' mean to you?" What it means to you may differ from what it means to me, and what it means to me may differ from what it means to someone else. Some may define the word "party" as a basic celebration. But what is the meaning of celebration? To some, it may mean drinking alcohol, consuming drugs, or spending time with friends. To others, celebration may mean engaging in any activity that provides joy and happiness. Some may say celebration means a grateful appreciation of life in general — a delight in the opportunity we have to be alive, and an expression of that delight in every moment of our day-to-day existence. I've preferred to leave my own definitions of "party" and "celebration" wide open, so that my understandings can grow and develop as much as possible. In the most basic sense, I've chosen to create music and art that reflect and create what I would call "physical and mental joy." With this, I hope to create enjoyable moments for myself and those around me, and to me, this type of joy has best been expressed through the word "party," which is direct and clear, but also open enough to allow as many people as possible the room to celebrate with me.

Now, someone may be saying, "Joy and celebration? What are those words doing in a book about Heavy Metal?" And some others may be saying, "What is Andrew W.K. doing in a book about Heavy Metal in the first place?" Here again, I'd like to point out that different people will have different understandings and ideas about what defines joy, and even what defines Heavy Metal. Aye Jay (the creator of this book) decided that it made perfect sense to have me in the book. That's why I was very honored and thankful when he asked if I would write this introduction. I was thrilled that he considered me part of this style of music he clearly loves, even if I had never considered myself to be a part of it. But again, what Aye Jay thinks of as "Heavy Metal" music may be very different from my own idea of it, and possibly different from yours as well. Just as every snowflake is unique, everyone's ideas about certain styles of music are as unique as imagination allows. Sure, it could be said that "Heavy Metal" means a certain sonic presentation, like, for example, distorted electric guitar. But does that mean all music featuring distorted guitar is "Heavy Metal"? Some may say yes and others no, and people may have different standards by which they classify music that go beyond the instruments used. Remember that the primary experience of listening to the music is that rush of excitement and good feelings we crave. Our ability to classify that experience, and label it as being "Heavy Metal" or "Rock" or "Good Music" or "Bad Music" is just a way for us to understand and make sense of an otherwise almost overwhelming amount of sensory information. I think it's okay to organize and label music, but I try to remember that these ideas are just labels, and not the music itself. Otherwise, we could satisfy our appetites by eating food descriptions and packaging, rather than consuming the flavors and nutrients found inside the food. The labels are our way of keeping track of a sensation, so that we may find it, or avoid it, more easily. Through this organization and preference, we're each able to decide on how a certain song or piece of music affects us, and most likely will continue to affect us, and then place it in a certain area of our own minds. This is the development of one's "taste." From that personalized taste, we're able to make preconceived choices about "what is what" and whether we like it or not. At the same time, it's my belief that a never-ending effort to appreciate ALL kinds of things, even what we decide we don't like, ultimately empowers us by adding to our lives, rather than taking away from our experiences and limiting ourselves. Without the vastness of all the different kinds of ideas and music, including what we "don't like," we wouldn't be able to form our own tastes in the first place, and pick and choose from all the world has to offer. Ultimately, understanding this can allow everyone to feel good by indulging in what we each love, and focusing on that love, rather than what feels bad and hateful.

In my opinion, true beauty is found in those vast differences, and in the undeniable similarities we experience with people, places, and things. With our actions and choices, we're giving genuine energy to our own ideas, and this energy either brings us together, or sets us apart. This energy is a surging and constant force — it's the same force that motivated Aye Jay to listen to the music that made him feel good, and the same force that helped him decide what he thinks "Heavy Metal" is, and make this book. Then, the energy from his actions created more of the same force, which in turn brought me in to write these words, and the same force compelling you to read them. I urge us all to embrace words like "energy," "force," and other ideas which may seem light and sentimental, and set aside our fears of being "unrealistic" or naive in believing in their power. For it is these illusive qualities and forces that we must hold onto tightest of all, and value for the mystery and wonder they inspire. It is these forces that give us goose bumps when a favorite riff starts on a song, and it is these forces that drive us to find more of those goose bumps. The energy in Heavy Metal music (whatever Heavy Metal music is) is the same energy that makes us tap our feet to drum beats, or bang our heads, or play instruments, or go to concerts, or look at books. Let us all develop and cherish our love for this energy, and let us realize that it's this energy — this force — that defines our love of Heavy Metal, and all of the great loves of our collective life.

PARTY HARD!
Love, Andrew W.K.

Color Rob Halford from Judas Priest

According to AC/DC, what is done dirt cheap?

Code:
26=a
25=b
24=c
23=d
22=e
21=f
20=g
19=h
18=i
17=j
16=k
15=l
14=m
13=n
12=o
11=p
10=q
9=r
8=s
7=t
6=u
5=v
4=w
3=x
2=y
1=z

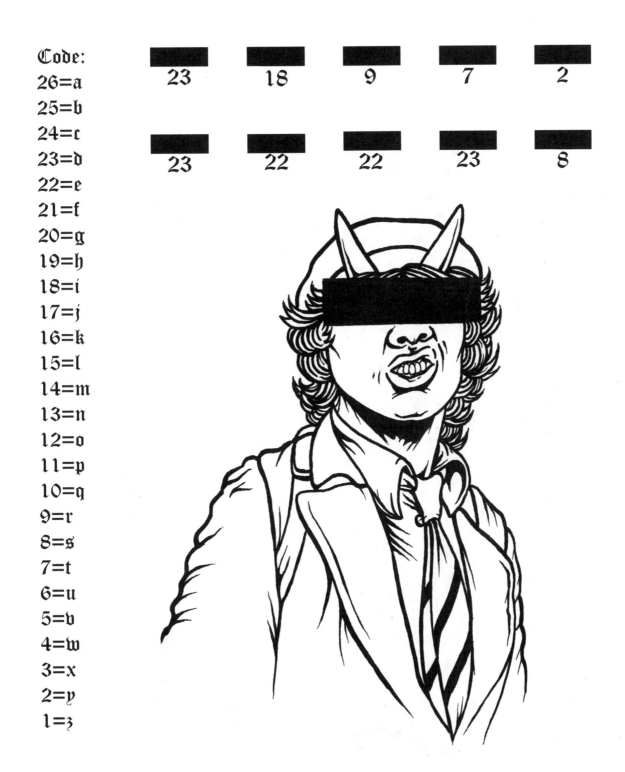

__23__ __18__ __9__ __7__ __2__

__23__ __22__ __22__ __23__ __8__

Finish drawing
Eddie from Iron Maiden

Hair Metal Crossword Puzzle

Fill in the blanks with the band who performed the songs listed below

Across

2. Youth Gone Wild
4. Edge of a Broken Heart
5. Alone Again
7. Love of a Lifetime
9. When the Children Cry
10. Once Bitten, Twice Shy
12. Girlschool
19. Cum on Feel the Noize
20. More than Words
22. House of Pain
24. To Hell with the Devil
25. Ballad of Jayne
26. Night Songs
29. Smooth Up
30. Rock You Like a Hurricane
31. Little Suzi

Down

1. Headed for a Heartbreak
3. Cherry Pie
5. Pour Some Sugar on Me
6. Round and Round
8. Up All Nite
11. We're Not Gonna Take It
13. Here I Go Again
14. Unskinny Bop
15. Kiss Me Deadly
16. Pissed
17. Fly High Michelle
18. Blind in Texas
21. Shout at the Devil
23. Freak Attack
27. After the Rain
28. The Final Countdown

Connect the moles to find out who this member of Motörhead is!

_ E M M Y

Heavy Metal Sudoku

Slayer match-up
Find the two matching logos

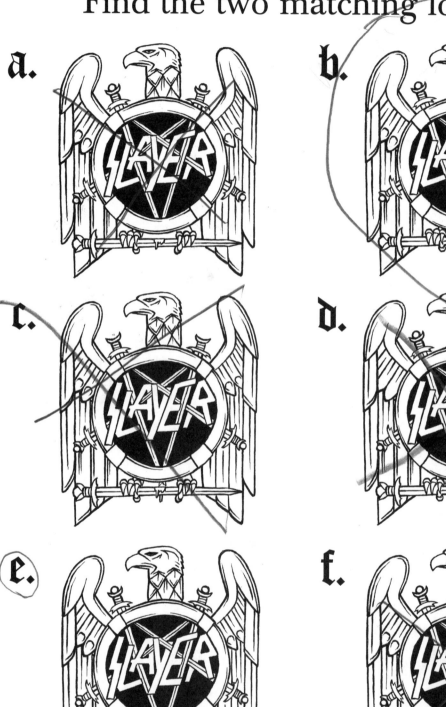

a.

b.

c.

d.

e.

f.

Color the shapes
marked with the dots
to see the hidden symbol

How many words can you make out of
White Zombie?

_____   _____

_____   _____

_____   _____

_____   _____

_____   _____

Backstage Maze
Help Spinal Tap through the backstage area!

Rock!!

Color Metallica (1983)

Color Metallica (1988)

Finish the drawing of Mortiis

Metal Pioneers Word Search

Cannibal Corpse
Angel Witch
Emperor
Sleep
Deep Purple

Armored Saint
Burzum
Blue Cheer
At the Gates
Kyuss

Krokus
Iced Earth
Celtic Frost
Venom
Death Angel

Entombed
Napalm Death
Dio
Carcass
Mercyful Fate

Deicide
Holocaust
Death
Voivod
Pentagram

```
W L H A N G E L W I T C H J Q X S O M M A R G A T N E P G Q
A F J B V C M S Z P C G F H G R D I C X T Z D H L V M A H L
C A G C E S P A D K H V Z B Q A D J H Y U C K O D O V I O V
A L K J H G E O H L S E Q A L M X V C T S D T L S M L J D W
N C F R D L R L K J H G F D S U W E R T U Q Y O F S R E M O
N S D F G L O F A F K J H B D C E Q W L P W U C D J K L N L
I W Q R T A R M O R E D S A I N T C F K S J O A P Y D S D B
B M P A T T H E G A T E S Q A D S B H J L O I U P E Y U C F
A D Q D R S A C G V H P Y U M N J M K E G U P S A S D C V D
L J E F B H J Z X C V B E F B N M I O G E T F T W E F G H E
C A S E W E R T Y U I J K N V A S S D Q Z R H A M N H J K A
O D F H P X C E R G T G H J S R T Y E S A S D F G V M L K T
R W E D Z P Z F S U K O R K N I W E R J H G U C M R D Z P H
P D F G B C U W E R Z A C K L N C B Y T R E W X E L O U Y A
S D F Z X O I R L A N Y N J J Y D E I C I D E N R M V G F N
E W F H B N K L P A W O M E C S D N D B S D W E C X L V U G
C O B F D S E W R L L O H F E S X T K E C M Y U Y L O D C E
R E C D S E A C V H E P O I V I B O U D A B E D F K P O E L
A T E J K I V R Y F D B C E J I K M W Z X R C J U K I Y E F
S C L W M U Z R U B V E N O M U I B X O I J T S L Z Q N M L
Q W T D F V E T Y U I O F A E Z R E A V B N J H F R E Q W E
A D I B A S D F O H M V B N P D A D S P O J B G A E S D F C
G A C S X C V G H Y U I J K B A S W E R F H K L T O U P M S
O P F N B C W Z X C V B N M E R L Z X C D A Q W E R T Y U L
A S R S D F K L O U H N I E R T Y M V B K O O I U T R E W Q
P A O X C V B H F T Y U R E S A N M D F D S T Y H J O I Y T
P O S I U S S A C R A C D S E R T Y U E V C D F G R D E W S
Q W T E R T Y U G B J K L L O U Y T R X A C V B D E W I A Z
Q W E R T Y U I O P A S D F G H J X B M K T T Y U H R S O C
S L E E P N M T Y E W S D F H J K L I P I Y H T S S U Y K J
```

17

Draw a line to identify the members of Guns 'n' Roses

1.

    W. Axl Rose

2.

    Izzy Stradlin

3.

    Duff McKagan

4.

    Slash

5.

    Steven Adler

Decline Match Game

Match the names to the quotes from the film
Decline of Western Civilization Part II: The Metal Years

1. Stephen Tyler, Aerosmith
2. Chris Holmes, W.A.S.P.
3. Ozzy Osbourne
4. Lemmy, Motörhead
5. Riki Rachtman

A. "We took LSD, we took cocaine, we took vast amounts of marijuana. It was fun at the time."

B. "I'm a full-blown alcoholic."

C. "It's a really big, fun, sleazy place."

D. "I must have snorted up all of Peru."

E. "I wish I was pretty."

How many words can you make out of Yngwie Malmsteen?

_____ _____

_____ _____

_____ _____

_____ _____

_____ _____

_____ _____

New Orleans Band Scramble

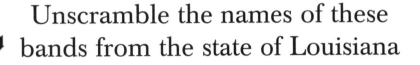

Unscramble the names of these
bands from the state of Louisiana

1. dteheoaeyg   ----------

2. idca tahb   ---- ----

3. rchtis nvrinosie   ------ ----------

4. arcorwb   -------

5. wnod   ----

6. hgtoawero   ---------

7. igcnpehraao   -----------

8. lsteion ernge   ------- -----

9. gikvin wcnro   ------ -----

10. jpusonirte tuirla   ---------- ------

Color the dotted shapes to find the inspiration behind bands like Sleep, Electric Wizard, High on Fire, Fu Manchu, Sons of Otis, Bongzilla and Queens of the Stone Age

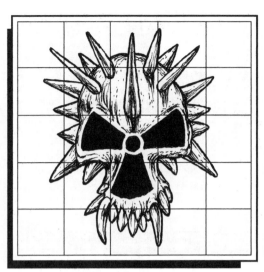

Use the grid to draw Corrosion of Conformity's logo

Holy Diver

You've been down too long in the _green_ sea
(adjective)

Oh what's _climB_ ing of me
(verb)

Ride the _BoB cat_
(animal)

You can see his _spots_ but you know he's clean
(feature of an animal)

Oh don't you _hear_ what I mean
(1 of the 5 senses)

Gotta get away

Holy Diver

Shiny _emrl_ s
(gemstone)

Like the eyes of a _Jaj._ in the _Pink_ and blue
(animal)   (color)

Something is _Smiling_ ing for you
(verb)

write for the morning
(verb)

You can hide in the _Moon_ 'till you see the light
(something in the sky)

Oh _pega_ will pray it's all right
(person)

Gotta get away – get away

Between the _saushy_ lies
(texture)

There's a truth that's _Burn_ as steel
(adjective)

The _Poop_ never dies
(noun)

putche 's a never-ending wheel
(noun)

Holy Diver

You're the _Gulf_ of the masquerade
(noun)

No need to _foot_ so afraid
(verb)

cat on the _Dog_
(verb)   (animal)

You can feel his _foox_ but you know he's mean
(animal's organ)

Some _Dho_ can never be seen
(noun)

Holy Diver

You've been down too long in the _Maastra_ sea
(adjective)

Oh what's _Caleri_ ing of me
(verb)

Ride the _Deth_ floop cuz
(animal)

You can see his _ear_ but you know he's clean
(part of an animal)

Oh don't you _Smell_ what I mean
(1 of the 5 senses)

Gotta get away – get away

Gotta get away – get away

Holy Diver

24

Connect the dots and color Dimebag Darrell's goatee

Van Halen Logo Match-Up
Find the two matching logos

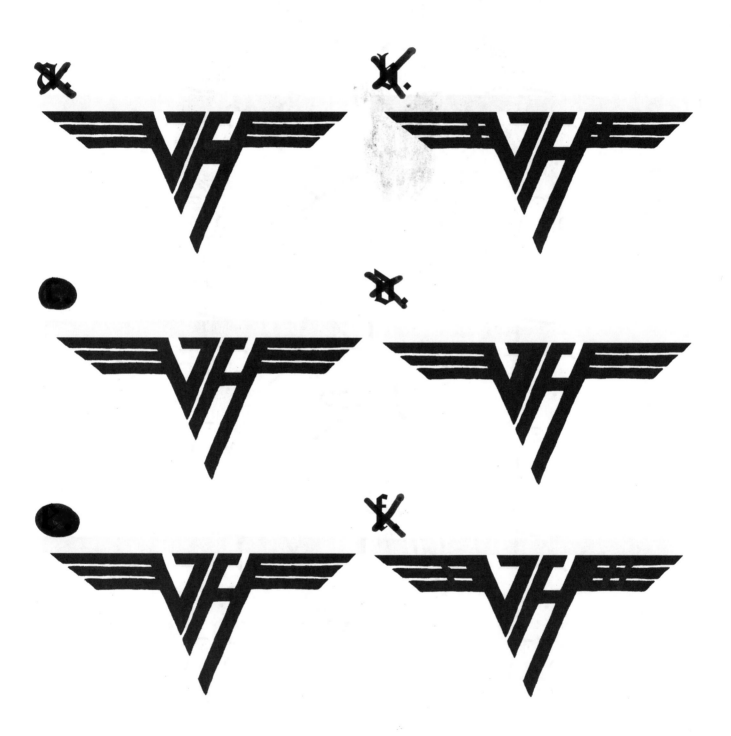

Draw yourself as Gene Simmons from KISS

Color Black Sabbath

Color Pantera

NEUROSIS

Song Title Word Search

Pain of Mind
Geneticide
Dominoes Fall
Obsequious Obsolescence
Tomorrow's Reality
The Road to Sovereignty
United Sheep
Souls at Zero
Sterile Vision
The Eye of Every Storm

Takeahnase
Enemy of the Sun
Raze the Stray
Lexicon
Through Silver in Blood
Rehumanize
Aeon
Times of Grace
Belief
A Sun That Never Sets

```
T F S D V E K P F Y Q L T F O E B A N G H O I Y I
G C V E F W S C V B K N H N Q C O G Y H B N Y M W
L O T A H G C X E B O D E O R E Z T A S L U O S Z
P J W Q M Q M N T O M O R R O W S R E A L I T Y K
A N M V C O R B N F C U O H B J A Q V E A Y I O H
V D S D M T O Q O T N U A U H P U S X U F A B Z H
H N O Y H Y T I U P U T D Y E I H I Y O S V Z Z B
Q S J N R N S T N S Z B T U O L C X Q U E V B E Y
B O Q A O W Y P X D X E O U I O L M N Z O X G O N
J E J S W I R Y A L C P S K N D S T W O N B A Y N
R T F E I L E B O A U O O Z V O H A G N I S N T B
I M P D V H V L R W B P V F G A Z K Z I M F E E L
D A A I H K E G K S Z L E J T S U E U B O V E A P
O E I C G E F I O R U S R N I M G A A K D I X V Z
B U N I D O O L B N I R E V L I S H G U O R H T G
W F O T S T E R I L E V I S I O N N E Z I C T L J
W F F E I S Y T K G E W G C C F U A D S I A Y D S
B L M N C X E A T R U U N V E A I S D E Y S F M S
M I I E T D E N S Y A R T S E H T E Z A R A S Y S
T F N G S W H E E N E M Y O F T H E S U N O Y T D
H C D H A R T X N D M I N Y X B J C C W Y K K S M
E Y E N F S N K O A S E L A A S X V D C O N H E C
U E Z I N A M U H E R A M Z D N R F F E G L Y Y I
P H G Q X Z J Y C B L A Y M I A F C L E O A E Y W
O H M Z K T J L R W N Y U J G C R M I B N Z W N B
```

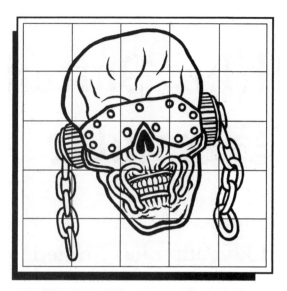

Use the grid to draw Megadeth's Vic Rattlehead

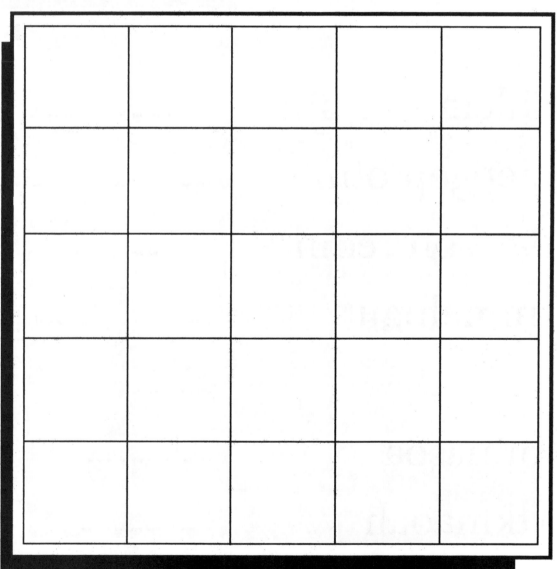

Mike Patton Scramble

Unscramble the names of bands
Mike Patton has fronted

1. phleimhacio   -----------

2. niepgep otm   ------- ---

3. tiahf on reom   ----- -- ----

4. rm nelbgu   -- ------

5. gevloa   ------

6. mtfnasoa   --------

7. wtkmaoah   --------

Sepultura Match
Circle the two matching logos

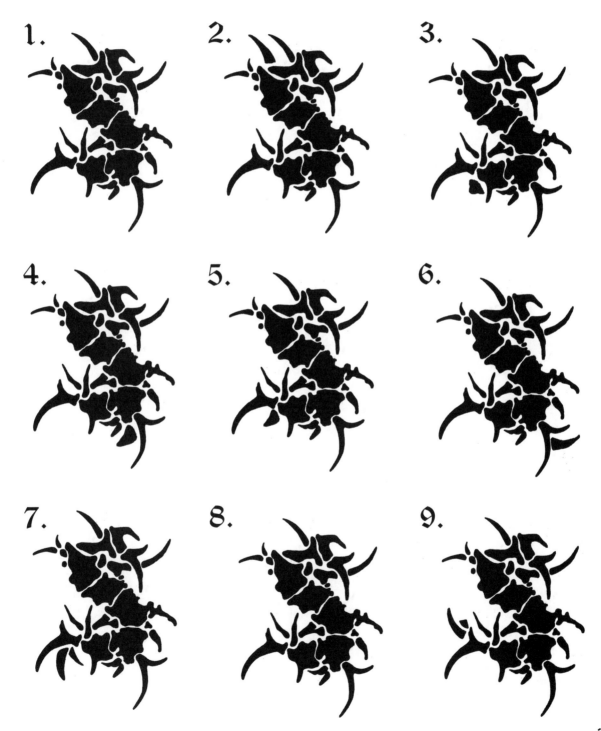

1.

2.

3.

4.

5.

6.

7.

8.

9.

TOOL Song Title Word Search

Hush
Lateralus
Parabola
Rosetta Stoned
Third Eye
Eulogy
Intension
Opiate

Part of Me
Sober
Faaip de Oiad
Jambi
Parabol
Prison Sex
Stinkfist
Undertow

```
Y N Q G E C P O V M F I X O K U C L Q T V A X W Q D E O P I
B W P H A M I M X U V A F G N S O H C U X R E G O V N X R X
G A M E N E A D D U P M Q A Z D E Q Z T P D G W P O L Y S I A
Q A E Y O L J E L I I P L I M U D Z C P R U Y U A F E D S S E
G I J U T C L Q C J V F R F P M N O C X D H P T N H K H O T
T R Q I M P T Q U A V R O H C D E O Z T O D E U C F U Q N Z
S Z O M P O D T K R I T J D D H E V I T H R K E M S G S S E
K Z Z J N K S V Z R U E C T M I O A S A I E Y G K B E E J
K E P T E O V J N P S R E J F A O E U A D E A D F M G Q C R O
K L H S W N Y G V A G H I K R O V L N D N T I E X D X A O Z
L V F G V K D O R R K B D G L V Q L A W V F N Q Y R Q S Z Y
H Y J O H S U A V M F B B L T S A B F X W E L I A A V I U L
T S I F K N I T S A S P D Z Z K A Q G T Z E L A A V I U L
U I Q S H U S H J L V T V E T C Y L X Y I R E L Y V Q Z H A
Z H Q R N O E Z W V O M O J I O F P P R X G C G K R O G N F
M A U W I H W H M X A F Y T T W G G A E X M V M O P I U O H
O Z N W N K L T I D G T I G P S R A R B Z X C U C F L X H V
M J O B X H M N F N P V Y P T A K F U A O H R Q O J I N M V
Q J U Y O R O S E T T A S T O N E D B S F O P W H Q S F Z Q
P C B Z P A R A B O L A M U L J W Q O Y X I Y J A G V K T T
K K P F Y W F E W Q P X V W G L P O F L O A R I G D G H O J Y
H O O B N P O O B M Z W A O C U V F T O T L U T G O J H V P Z
T X O Z J F B B P U E S T Z S O D Q W E H C C U W S L Q M H E
Y Z L U G C C Y Q Y A V S R F O S M M A O L L V J Q K U U E
T N W X Q M K D P T G X E N R A N K T N W X D A P E A E N L
N K N W X D B H P D V P D B R O W H N D U B E Z M C F A F
R M H K Z J D I C M L I N Y H A W W X F D G Y N Y S E E F I
R C W E Q E D F V R M U U S J P C Z H E T C X M L J N O I X
V D Y E P O L K Z J J T R G E I N K U L K B F O I C D V O H
```

Connect Buzz from the Melvins

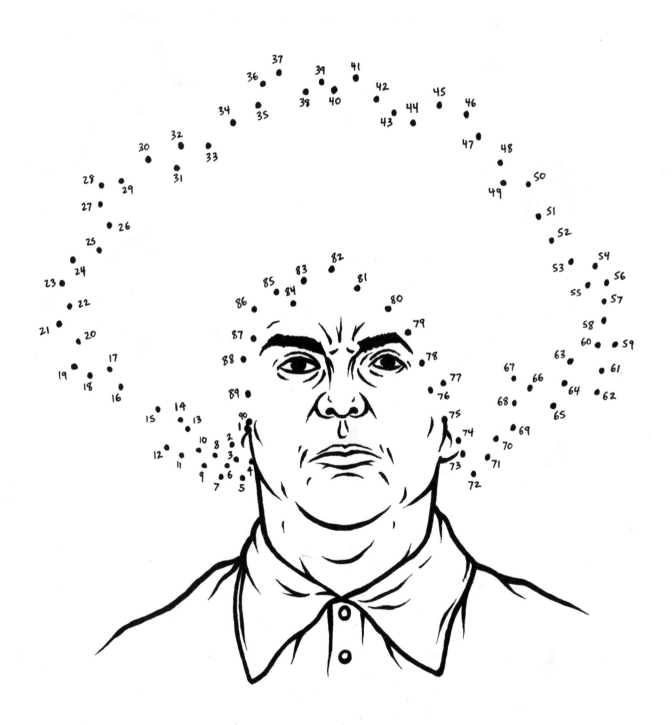

Color Andrew W.K.

Use the maze to help Ozzy Osbourne get to Ozzfest

Ozzfest

Color Glenn Danzig

Monsters of Rock Crossword

Across

4. Athens-based band named after gay rights activist
7. Band led by wino; not the Obsessed
9. Boston doom metal band who put out music on Southern Lord records
11. Band's self-titled debut was also known as *Psalm 9*
12. Kill All Redneck Pricks
13. Australian doom metal pioneers
19. "Brutal death metal" band signed to Roadrunner Records
20. True Sounds Of Liberty
21. South Carolina band inspired by ancient Egypt
22. Stormtroopers Of Death
23. Rockville, Maryland, band fronted by Wino

Down

1. Dirty Rotten Imbeciles
2. This band's album *Will to Mangle* produced by Billy Anderson
3. Tampa, Florida, band originally named "Xecutioner"
5. Texas-based thrash metal band
6. The antithesis of utopia
8. English sludge band signed to Earache Records
10. Swedish doom metal band
14. Along with Paradise Lost and Anathema, part of North England's "great three"
15. Death metal band named after weapon in roleplaying game
16. Band named after line in a Dr. Seuss book
17. Bay area band that included a pre-Primus Larry LaLonde on guitar
18. Band formed in 1989 after Lee Dorrian left Napalm Death

Use the grid to draw Anthrax's "not" man

Led Zeppelin Match
Draw a line to match the symbol to the member of the band that it represents

1.

Robert Plant

2.

John Bonham

3.

Jimmy Page

4.

John Paul Jones

Black Metal Band Word Scramble

1. pmroere   _ _ _ _ _ _ _

2. horgotgro   _ _ _ _ _ _ _ _ _

3. ymhame   _ _ _ _ _ _

4. terkdhrano   _ _ _ _ _ _ _ _ _ _

5. nmoev   _ _ _ _ _

6. yohabrt   _ _ _ _ _ _ _

7. urubmz   _ _ _ _ _ _

8. rakd fneulra   _ _ _ _   _ _ _ _ _ _ _

9. lmtmaroi   _ _ _ _ _ _ _ _

10. tmauprbu   _ _ _ _ _ _ _ _

11. taown   _ _ _ _ _

12. lmarelehmh   _ _ _ _ _ _ _ _ _ _

Slipknot Numbers Game

Draw lines to match the members to the numbers 0-8

0 1 2 3 4 5 6 7 8

a.

b.

c.

d.

e.

f.

g.

h.

i.

Color GWAR

Connect the dots to see what letter "flies"

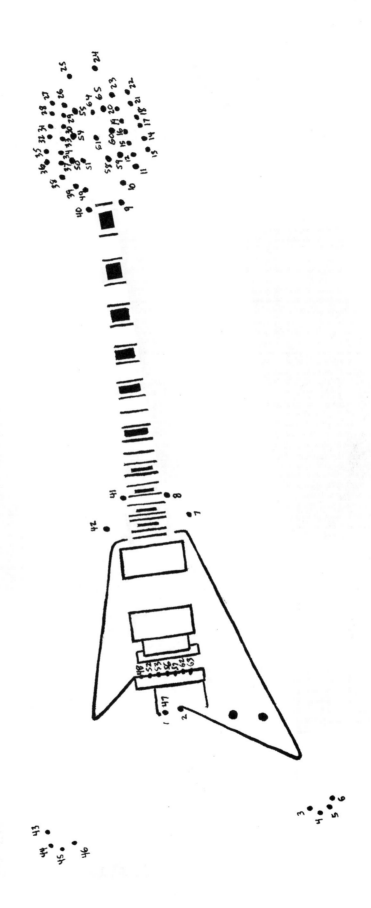

How many words can you make out of Al Jourgensen?*

_____ _____

_____ _____

_____ _____

_____ _____

_____ _____

_____ _____

* of Ministry

Answers

Pg. 5, AC/DC game: Dirty Deeds

Pg. 7, Hair Metal Crossword:
ACROSS: 2. Skid Row, 4. Vixen, 5. Dokken,
7. Firehouse, 9. White Lion, 10. Great White,
12. Britny Fox, 19. Quiet Riot, 20. Extreme,
22. Faster Pussycat, 24. Stryper, 25. L.A. Guns,
26. Cinderella, 29. BulletBoys, 30. Scorpions,
31. Tesla
DOWN: 1. Winger, 3. Warrant, 5. Def Leppard,
6. Ratt, 8. Slaughter, 11. Twisted Sister,
13. Whitesnake, 14. Poison, 15. Lita Ford,
16. Dangerous Toys, 17. Enuff Z'nuff, 18. W.A.S.P.,
21. Mötley Crüe, 23. Lynch Mob, 27. Nelson,
28. Europe

Pg. 10, Slayer Match: b & e

Pg. 18, Guns 'n' Roses Match: 1-Slash, 2-Adler,
3-Axl, 4-Duff, 5-Izzy

Pg. 19, Decline Match: 1-d, 2-b, 3-a, 4-e, 5-c

Pg. 21, New Orleans Scramble: 1. Eyehategod,
2. Acid Bath, 3. Christ Inversion, 4. Crowbar,
5. Down, 6. Goatwhore, 7. Necrophagia,
8. Soilent Green, 9. Viking Crown,
11. Superjoint Ritual

Pg. 26, Van Halen Match: c & e

Pg. 32, Mike Patton Scramble: 1. Hemophiliac,
2. Peeping Tom, 3. Faith No More, 4. Mr Bungle,
5. Lovage, 6. Fantomas, 7. Tomahawk

Pg. 33, Sepultura Match: 1 & 8

Pg. 39, Monsters of Rock Crossword:
ACROSS: 4. Harvey Milk, 7. Saint Vitus,
9. Grief, 11. Trouble, 12. Karp,
13. Disembowelment, 19. Suffocation,
20. T.S.O.L., 21. Nile, 22. S.O.D.,
23. The Obsessed
DOWN: 1. D.R.I., 2. Sourvein, 3. Obituary,
5. Rigor Mortis, 6. Dystopia, 8. Iron Monkey,
10. Candlemass, 14. My Dying Bride, 15. Bolt
Thrower, 16. Noothgrush, 17. Possessed,
18. Cathedral

Pg. 41, Zeppelin Match: 1-Page, 2-Plant,
3-Jones, 4-Bonham

Pg. 42, Black Metal Scramble: 1. Emperor,
2. Gorgoroth, 3. Mayhem, 4. Darkthrone,
5. Venom, 6. Bathory, 7. Burzum, 8. Dark
Funeral, 9. Immortal, 10. Abruptum, 11. Wotan,
12. Hellhammer

Pg. 43, Slipknot Numbers Game: a-4, b-2, c-6,
d-8, e-3, f-1, g-5, h-7, i-0

Contributors

www.burlesquedesign.com

www.andrewwk.com

www.egotripland.com

www.ayejay.com

THANK YOU: Meka, Greta and Cohen; every one of the artists in the book; the heavy metal photographers and visual artists; The Dream Team: Horkey for the letters, Brent for the design, and Andrew for the foreword; the metal experts that helped me shape the book with their invaluable advice: Matt Loomis, Jeremy Golden, Letta Wren Christianson, Mike Fisher, Aaron, Paul Townsend, Martin Popoff, and Wezz Winship.

Thank you also: Larry & Lucretia Klungtvet; The Moranos; Jean Fusco; everyone at ECW; Wendy and Ronnie James Dio; Brendon & Metalocolypse; Burlesque design; Mike 2600; Pushead; Glen E. Friedman; Doug Surreal; Todd Bratrud; George Thompson; Nathan and Foundation skateboards; Ron, Colin, Bucky, Chris, and Anna at Last Gasp; Aaron Turner; Edan; Heathakilla; Faydog; Seldon Hunt; B+; Fred Armisen; Mike Patton; Ian MacKaye; Karp; Shawna Gore; Trench; Buzzwurm; Kevin Boettcher; Timmy Smith; Fitz of Depression; Henry & Chunklet magazine; Steve Albini; Josh & Generica; Jim Rizzuto; Kelly O & the Stranger; Juxtapoz; Matt Sonzala; Z-man; Fecal Face dot com; Faesthetic; Albert Reyes; Andy Howell; Andrew Pommier; Anthony Ausgang; Attaboy; Barry McGee; Bigfoot; Buffmonster; Art Chantry; No Pattern; Jon Burgerman; Crash; Kaws; KR; Charles Burns; Charles Krafft; Devi; Chris Ware; Cody Hudson; Dave Choe; David Horvath & Sun Min-Kim; Dave Kinsey; David Flores; Doze Green; Frank Kozik; Gary Baseman; Gary Panter; Gary Taxali; Haze; Isabell Samaras & Nico; Jad Fair; Jason Brunson; Jeremy Fish; Jim Mafood; Johnny Ryan; John Stewart; Junko Mizunko; The London Police; Mark Gonzales; Mark Ryden; Michael Leon; KRK Ryden; Mark Dean Veca; Mike Giant; Mike Aho; Marion Peck; Ramm:El:Zee; Rich Jacobs; Rob Reger; Jesse LeDoux; Ryan Jacob Smith; Sam Henderson; Seizer; M. Sebien; Shepard Fairey; Tiffany Bozic; Travis Millard; Mel Kadel; Tim Biskup; The Pizz; Upso; Winston Smith; Aiyana Udesen, Jason Goad, the city of Chico; and anyone else I may have forgotten.

Thanks again!